Figures of Speech

A Study and Practice Guide

Written by R.E. Myers

Illustrated by Bron Smith

Teaching & Learning Company
1204 Buchanan St., P.O. Box 10
Carthage, IL 62321-0010

This book belongs to

_____

Copyright © 2008, Teaching & Learning Company

ISBN No. 13: 978-1-57310-563-7

Printing No. 987654321

Teaching & Learning Company
1204 Buchanan St., P.O. Box 10
Carthage, IL 62321-0010

The purchase of this book entitles teachers to make copies for use in their individual classrooms only. This book, or any part of it, may not be reproduced in any form for any other purposes without prior written permission from the Teaching & Learning Company. It is strictly prohibited to reproduce any part of this book for an entire school or school district, or for commercial resale. The above permission is exclusive of the cover art, which may not be reproduced.

All rights reserved. Printed in the United States of America.

Table of Contents

Lesson 1	Tracy Was Mad (Similes)	5
Lesson 2	Like What? (Similes)	7
Lesson 3	One Thing Is Another (Metaphors)	10
Lesson 4	Metaphorical Expressions (Metaphors)	13
Lesson 5	Fins Beat Feathers (Idioms)	16
Lesson 6	Not to Be Taken Literally (Idioms)	18
Lesson 7	All About Alliteration (Alliteration)	20
Lesson 8	The Money-Making Mayor (Alliteration)	23
Lesson 9	Hink-Pinks (Rhyme)	26
Lesson 10	Wise 'n' Rhymers (Rhyme)	28
Lesson 11	Quick Milk (Puns, Riddles)	30
Lesson 12	The Paws That Refreshes (Puns)	32
Lesson 13	But Who's the Father? (Personification, Maxims)	36
Lesson 14	Some Persons Who Aren't (Personification)	38
Lesson 15	Losing in Order to Win (Paradoxes, Anecdotes)	40
Lesson 16	Make Mine Candy (Irony, Cinquains)	44
Lesson 17	Whistling Cops (Analogies)	46
Lesson 18	Apt Comparisons (Analogies)	49
Lesson 19	The Handsome Stranger (Hyperbole)	52
Lesson 20	Tall Tales (Hyperbole)	55
Lesson 21	Click, Hiss, Honk and Coo (Onomatopoeia)	58
Lesson 22	Part or Whole? (Synecdoche)	60
Lesson 23	Not Bad (Litotes)	62
Lesson 24	One Mixed-Up Man (Spoonerisms)	64
Lesson 25	Jake's Fright (Spoonerisms, Alliteration)	66
Lesson 26	Repeaters (Tautologies)	68
Lesson 27	Game Shows (Malapropisms)	70
Lesson 28	Abbreviations (Acronyms)	72
Lesson 29	What Does It Mean? (Review of Figurative Language)	76

Introduction

Figures of Speech is only about—surprise!—figures of speech. It focuses upon literary devices or techniques to spice up and invigorate prose and poetry. Among the included devices are *simile, metaphor, paradox, irony, litotes, synecdoche* and *alliteration* which will introduce new vocabulary as part of the creative learning.

The methodology for each lesson is to give a definition, offer some examples and have the student practice using the figure of speech. The approach throughout is to combine convergent and divergent thinking—or, in Bloom's terminology—comprehension, application and synthesis.

Improving the writing skills of middle school students in grades 5-9 has been, and will continue to be, an ongoing educational priority. It's a time when young people are expanding their spoken vocabulary and language skills; the written process should be as pleasant and enjoyable as the verbal part.

Good writing doesn't depend upon tricks to be worthwhile, but skillful writers use devices and techniques to make their work more enjoyable and understandable. Though middle schoolers may be adept at verbally using similes and metaphors, they are probably not adept at including them in their writing. After learning about the techniques in *Figures of Speech*, students will hopefully use the techniques so that they are proud of their writing.

Teacher tips have been included because some teachers will benefit from pointers about preparing, presenting and following through with the lessons. For those who prefer to use their inherent background of knowledge and ignore the teacher guide material, go for it!

Reference: Espey, W.R. *The Garden of Eloquence.* New York: Harper, 1983.

Tracy Was Mad
Identifying Similes

Lesson 1

Teacher Tips

It is likely that students use similes more than any other figure of speech. As we know, common similes are used so often that they constitute one of the largest groups of cliches. In this lesson, students are to identify four of those trite similes in a short story and then use them in sentences. All similes don't have to be hackneyed, this should be pointed out.

Introduction

Lead into the lesson by asking students to fill in a few of these expressions:

blind as _____

_____ as a tack

smart as _____

like taking candy from _____

hungry as _____

_____ as a doornail

sicker than _____

like shooting fish in _____

like making a mountain out of _____

Substitute others if you believe these similes are not readily recognizable by your students.

Follow Through

The similes in the story about Tracy on page 6 are shown in this order:
1. as mad as a wet hen
2. shake like a leaf
3. Quicker than you can say "Jack Robinson"
4. make his ears ring like that cymbal
5. fell like a ton of bricks

"Make his ears ring like that cymbal" is not a trite simile. Encourage your students to be original.

Targeted Outcomes

- Identify five similes in a short story.
- Use four of the similes in sentences.

Name_____

Tracy Was Mad

A. If you hear someone say that a friend is "happy as a lark," you aren't likely to think, "Oh, that's a simile." But that's the name we give to expressions that compare things and use *as, like* and *than*. They are commonly heard, and denote a common characteristic. **A simile, then, is a figure of speech in which two unlike things are compared and has the words *as, like* or *than*.**

B. Identify five similes in the following paragraphs by underlining them.

Tracy was as mad as a wet hen! She had told her brother she needed her car at 3:00 so she could meet Whitney at the mall, and here it was 3:30 and he hadn't come back. Tracy wasn't able to let Whitney know why she was late because Whitney didn't have a cell phone. Her father took it away from her because Whitney ran up such a whopping bill last month.

Tracy's father had threatened to do the same with her cell phone. That had made her shake like a leaf because she wouldn't be the same person without her cell phone. Fortunately, Tracy's mother had intervened, telling her husband if he did that it wouldn't be very pleasant in the house. Quicker than you can say "Jack Robinson," the old guy gave in.

If Kyle ever showed up, she'd make his ears ring like that cymbal he was always hitting when he practiced his drums. Kyle was usually dependable, but lately his head was in the clouds. He'd fallen like a ton of bricks for Krista. Who could get sillier over a girl than her brother?

C. Four of the similes in the passage are used very often in common speech. Write them below; then use each simile in a sentence.

Simile #1:_____

_____

Simile #2:_____

_____

Simile #3:_____

_____

Simile #4:_____

_____

Like What?
Produce 12 Original Similes
Compile a List of Colorful and Effective Expressions

Lesson 2

Teacher Tips

"Like What?" can be most effectively introduced after a student has used a colorful expression in class. If you're fortunate to have students who frequently express themselves in unusual or quaint ways, your class will be aware of the attention-getting value of such language. However, if your students uniformly adopt current cliches, this lesson might follow up a colorful phrase read in a book. Teachers regularly attack the problem of "tired" language, and "Like What?" is well suited to illustrating how much more interesting speech can be when we abandon well-worn conversational devices.

The "warming up" activity offers an opportunity to point out how routinely we use the expressions that come to mind quickly; we have to hesitate a little not to say "sharp as a tack" or "stubborn as a mule." Ask, "What comes after 'sells like _____'?" Students will probably say "hot cakes," and this will enable you to point out how much more interesting language can be when we avoid trite expressions and use vivid, thought-provoking words and phrases. It will also enable you to show how new and fresh analogies can lead to more honest expression. After all, hot cakes are not always best-sellers.

Part two of the lesson asks students to consider reasons for copycat language. Why do people tend to talk in the same manner as those around them? Students will likely begin to become more self-conscious about their own speaking and writing habits.

Follow Through

Note whether students can recognize similes, metaphors and other figures of speech in works they read. After completing this lesson, they should be better able to recognize a simile and other figures of speech.

A useful exercise to test this type of progress is to have students describe a photograph or painting so others can see the picture through the words of the writer or speaker.

Targeted Outcomes

- Complete 12 similes.
- Consider how language as a basic tool of communication has evolved.
- Compile a list of colorful and effective expressions.

Name_____

Lesson 2
Similes

Like What?

A. Have you ever heard expressions such as "sharp as a tack" or "snug as a bug in a rug"? Or "That's like trying to find a needle in a haystack"? When we talk like that we are using similes. Similes point out likenesses or similarities in things. You will find the words *as, like* or *than* in a simile; *as* and *like* are most often used when we make comparisons.

In this activity think of unusual and colorful ways to compare things. Part of a simile is given; you are to complete it with words of your own. For example, if you were given "clear as _____," you could supply an ending such as "a mountain stream in spring." The usual ways to use *clear* as the beginning of a simile are to say or write "clear as a bell" or "clear as crystal," but you are to think of other ways to convey the ideas.

1. pretty as a _____

2. like stealing _____

3. rough as _____

4. straight as _____

5. smooth as _____

6. black as _____

7. like rolling _____

8. crazy as _____

9. slippery as _____

10. _____ as the day is long

11. nervous as _____

12. straight as _____

Let's reverse the process.
Can you think of an adjective that fits a puppy?

like a puppy or _____ as a puppy.

B. Many expressions are heard and used so often that they no longer have much effect upon our ears. Why do you suppose so many of us use the same expressions over and over again?

_____

_____

Name_____

Like What?

What suggestions do you have for making language more colorful and more meaningful?

_____

_____

_____

_____

_____

_____

_____

C. In the space below, record expressions you hear and read that you believe are particularly colorful or effective. Sources for an informal survey of picturesque language are almost limitless. "Monitor" the speech of your classmates, salespeople, television personalities, people in public places, your parents and relatives, newspaper reporters, magazine writers, authors, poets and so on. Monitor your own speech. You might want to keep on adding to your list of expressions for several weeks. You will probably be surprised to learn where the best sources of colorful expressions come from.

_____

_____

_____

_____

_____

_____

_____

_____

_____

_____

Lesson 3

One Thing Is Another
Identifying Metaphors

Teacher Tips

Metaphors tend to go unnoticed because many of them are common expressions in our everyday language. Expressions such as "It was an accident waiting to happen," and "Gary's mind was a sponge that soaked up knowledge at an amazing rate" are so common that they don't seem to be figures of speech at all.

This lesson is comprised of a definition of a metaphor, two exercises requiring students to identify metaphors, and then being asked to create three sentences with their own metaphors.

Begin the lesson distinguishing between a metaphor and a simile. If the example of Jerry's working like a horse isn't clear, please select one of your own to show the difference between a simile and a metaphor.

Evaluating Responses

In the first exercise with sentences on page 12, students underline the metaphors:

1. Jane's mother was an island of comfort during those dark days.
2. They nipped his idea in the bud.
3. That sly old fox got his way again.
4. "Noah is a straight arrow, all right—he keeps us out of trouble," commented Robbie.
5. A wave of gloom engulfed the expedition.
6. His career was a comet that would end in the inevitable crash.
7. Day after day, the ship just plowed the waves.

These metaphors are found in the passage about Randolph on page 12:

1. A loose cannon
2. Harry shot a furtive glance
3. to catch his eye
4. thundered Randolph
5. his angry words pressed sickeningly on each man's head

One Thing Is Another
Identifying Metaphors

Lesson 3

The distinction between a metaphor and an idiom is often quite difficult to make. If a student composes a sentence in the last part of the lesson such as "With a great deal of skill, Nancy nailed down the agreement," you will probably want to allow it to pass as a metaphor. Frequently metaphors and idioms are identical. Since Nancy's behavior wasn't literally an act of hitting a nail, the expression is a metaphor that compares her success dealing with the agreement to the action of a hammer driving a nail down all the way into a board. On the other hand, "nailing down the agreement" is also an idiom in that it is an accepted expression that isn't to be taken literally. Both figures of speech are so familiar that they are instantly understood by the listener or reader.

Targeted Outcomes

- Identify metaphors in seven sentences.
- Identify metaphors in a passage.
- Compose three sentences with metaphors.

Name_____

One Thing Is Another

Lesson 3
Metaphors

A. **A metaphor is an implied comparison in which a word or phrase used for one thing is applied in place of another.** Metaphors aren't introduced by *as* or *like*, as similes are. For example, if you say "Jerry works as hard as a horse in the fields," you are using a metaphor; but if you say "Jerry works like a horse in the fields," you are using a simile.

B. Following are some common metaphors. Underline them.

1. Jane's mother was an island of comfort during those dark days.

2. They nipped his idea in the bud.

3. That sly old fox got his way again.

4. "Noah is a straight arrow, all right—he keeps us out of trouble," commented Robbie.

5. A wave of gloom engulfed the expedition.

6. His career was a comet that would end in the inevitable crash.

7. Day after day, the ship just plowed the waves.

All the metaphors in the sentences above are used so often that they are also cliches; that is, they are tired expressions that seem to come automatically to our lips.

C. Underline the five metaphors in the following passage:

Randolph's expression was murderous. A loose cannon, he was one dangerous man when he got in that black mood. The others cowered in a corner of the smoke-filled room. Harry shot a furtive glance in Randolph's direction, but was careful not to catch his eye.

Well, what are we going to do about that brute?" thundered Randolph.

The silence that followed his angry words pressed sickeningly on each man's head until they felt like yelling . . . but were afraid to.

D. Write three sentences that each contain a metaphor.

1. _____
_____

2. _____
_____

3. _____
_____

Metaphorical Expressions
Learning About Metaphors

Lesson 4

Teacher Tips

After discussing similes and metaphors, this lesson has students discriminating between similes and metaphors. Another exercise has them converting similes into metaphors.

In most instances, students will have no difficulty picking out the similes. Although similes with *than* are not used as frequently as similes with *as* and *like*, we do have a fair number of them ("hotter than blazes," "dumber than a doorknob," "nuttier than a fruitcake," etc.).

Evaluating Responses

Similes and metaphors should be listed as shown below.

Similes	Metaphors
slower than molasses in January	With the heart of a lion
clear as a bell	triumph was written all over his face
slippery as an eel	Wilson was the bulldog
happy as a tick in a fat dog	injected steel into his flaccid spine
like a chicken with its head cut off	the king of the household

These are ways that the sentences with similes can be converted to sentences with metaphors:

1. Fred was a trusted shepherd taking care of that swarm of little boys.
2. "Don't be a bump on a log, Everett," Mrs. Norris complained to her husband.
3. He was always a lone wolf in his dealings.
4. Our office is a circus these days, and the clowns are in charge.
5. The river was a ribbon of moonlight.
6. A filthy drowned rat, Stephen lay on the banks of the river after the flood.
7. The building was a tomb of silence after the rowdy people left.
8. You couldn't be uneasy in Mr. Gully's presence because he was just an old shoe.
9. Tony is an iceberg when it comes to revealing his feelings about that.
10. Kim is an agile bunny the way she darts around the tennis court.

Any sentence that produces a legitimate metaphor is satisfactory.

Targeted Outcomes

- Identify five similes and five metaphors in a group of 10 sentences.
- Convert five similes into metaphors in 10 additional sentences.

Name_____

Lesson 4 Metaphors

Metaphorical Expressions

A. The two most common figures of speech are similes and metaphors. They both make comparisons, but similes are more direct and they have the words *like, as* and *than*. Metaphors bring out similarities in completely different things by calling one thing another, as in "At the table, Sarah was a timid little mouse who was afraid she'd squeak at the wrong time." **A metaphor is defined as "an implied comparison in which a word or phrase used for one thing is applied in place of another."**

B. Here are 10 sentences that contain similes and metaphors. Put an S in the blank in front of the similes and an M in front of the metaphors.

_____ 1. With the heart of a lion, Jon Nord scattered the rioters in every direction.

_____ 2. When it came to doing his chores, Reggie was slower than molasses in January.

_____ 3. As he crossed the finish line, triumph was written all over his face.

_____ 4. Her voice came down from above, clear as a bell.

_____ 5. Wilson was the bulldog of Ashbury Park, always steadfast and fierce in protecting the weak, innocent and downtrodden.

_____ 6. With just those few words, she seemed to inject steel into his flaccid spine.

_____ 7. All that day Clem was as happy as a tick on a fat dog.

_____ 8. He was running around like a chicken with its head cut off.

_____ 9. The cat rose on its haunches and looked directly ahead—without a doubt, the acknowledged king of the household.

_____ 10. That Ned—he's slippery as an eel!" exclaimed Nell.

14 TLC10563 Copyright © Teaching & Learning Company, Carthage, IL 62321-0010

Name_____

Metaphorical Expressions

Lesson 4
Metaphors

C. Below are 10 sentences that contain similes. Change each one so that the sentence contains a metaphor instead of a simile. For example, a sentence reading "Melanie talks like a magpie when she's among her friends" can be changed to "Melanie certainly is a magpie when she's among her friends." Since the first sentence compares Melanie to a magpie and uses *like*, it is a simile. The second sentence doesn't have *like*, but it makes the same comparison and therefore contains a metaphor.

1. Fred was like a trusted shepherd taking care of that swarm of little boys.

   _____

2. "Don't sit there like a bump on a log, Everett," Mrs. Norris complained to her husband.

   _____

3. He always operated like a lone wolf in his dealings.

   _____

4. Our office is like a circus these days, and the clowns are in charge.

   _____

5. Like a ribbon of moonlight, the river reflected the glow of the moon.

   _____

6. Not moving, he lay like a filthy, drowned rat on the banks of the river after the flood.

   _____

7. The building was as silent as a tomb after the rowdy people left.

   _____

8. Because Mr. Gully was as comfortable as an old shoe, you couldn't be uneasy in his presence.

   _____

9. When it comes to revealing his feelings about that, Tony is as cold as an iceberg.

   _____

10. Kim darts around the tennis court like an agile bunny.

    _____

Fins Beat Feathers
Identifying Idioms

Lesson 5

Teacher Tips

Idioms tend to go unnoticed because they are common expressions in everyday language. Expressions such as "Her eyes flew to the guilty party," "With a great deal of skill, he nailed down the agreement," and "Eyes bulging, the coach steamed on to the playing field" are so common that they don't seem to be figures of speech at all.

Evaluating Responses

The six idioms in the story on page 17 are:

1. The Barracudas <u>Take a Bite Out of the Eagles</u> (the title)
2. Bo was able <u>to bull his way</u>
3. the Barracudas just <u>ran roughshod</u> over the Eagles
4. the Eagles <u>were swamped</u>, 48-0
5. they didn't want <u>to grind the Eagles' noses</u>
6. The Barracudas <u>had gone down that road</u>

Targeted Outcomes

- Identify six idioms in a story.

Name_____

Fins Beat Feathers

You may not realize that you and your friends use **idioms** in ordinary conversation. If you say, "The days flew by during our vacation" or "Mindy just blew her out of the water with that one," you are using an idiom. **An idiom is an expression that has a meaning different from the literal words it uses.** If taken literally, an idiom is not true, as in "He went to pieces when he heard the terrible news." (The person was greatly affected by the news, but he didn't actually break into pieces.)

Underline the six idioms in this paragraph about two high school football teams.

The Barracudas Take a Bite Out of the Eagles

The game wasn't very thrilling. Bo Hardisty and his teammates controlled the line of scrimmage, and Bo was able to bull his way to four touchdowns. In fact, the Barracudas just ran roughshod over the Eagles in the third quarter. The coach of the Barracudas put in his second- and third-stringers in the fourth quarter to at least show a little mercy, but by then the Eagles were swamped, 48-0. After the game was over, however, the Barracudas were gracious in victory; they didn't want to grind the Eagles' noses in defeat. The Barracudas had gone down that road earlier in the season, and it was no fun.

Lesson 6
Not to Be Taken Literally
Recognizing Idioms

Teacher Tips

This lesson about idioms is comprised of a definition, some examples and an exercise that allows your students to demonstrate their ability to recognize an idiom when they see (or hear) one. If we are successful in putting over the idea of what this figure of speech is, your students should be more aware of the important role idioms play in our language.

Evaluating Responses

There are six idioms in the story about Luke and Jeremy on page 19.

1. Jeremy <u>threaded his way</u> . . .
2. Luke <u>was beside himself</u> with excitement.
3. . . . <u>threw an amused look</u> . . .
4. He hesitated, <u>fighting with himself</u>.
5. . . . and <u>throw cold water</u> . . .
6. <u>Luke's face fell</u> . . .

You might find that the last idiom escapes some of your students, but a "face falling" is truly an idiomatic expression.

Targeted Outcomes

- Learn the definition of an idiom.
- Be able to identify six idioms in a little story.

Name_____

Lesson 6
Idioms
Not to Be Taken Literally

A. **An idiom is an accepted phrase, construction or expression that is contrary to the usual patterns of language and has a different meaning from the literal words.** For example, suppose a man is fired from his job. We can say that he is then in low spirits, or we can say he is "down in the dumps." The man doesn't go to the city dump, of course; "down in the dumps" is just an idiomatic expression that describes his depression.

B. These are other sayings that aren't meant to be taken literally but which instantly convey their meanings because they are used so often:
- Tom flew off the handle more than ever back then.
- Marge sang a different tune when she heard the family was rich.
- He was all at sea in trying to understand the document.
- "Don't make a pig of yourself," admonished Tim's mother.
- She ran circles around him.
- "Don't beat about the bush—tell me what's on your mind," Melvin said.
- Philip Ransome blazed a new trail in science with his discovery.
- The judge threw the book at Orville.
- It's no wonder she's exhausted—she's always burning the candle at both ends.
- "Look at Felix lagging behind there; I'm afraid he's run out of gas," remarked the coach.
- We don't want to do business with them—they don't operate on a level playing field.

All of the sentences above contain idioms, and because we use them so often they are also cliches, that is, expressions that are so common they are stale.

C. Underline the idioms in this story:

Six-year-old Luke yelled at his friend Jeremy to come over to the pond and see what he had found. Jeremy threaded his way through the thick reeds and soggy ground and finally reached Luke's side.

"Look there, Jeremy! It has legs and a tail, and it swims like a fish. I'll bet it's a new kind of animal!"

Luke was beside himself with excitement.

Jeremy gazed at the creature and then threw an amused look at his young friend. He hesitated, fighting with himself as to whether he should tell Luke the truth and throw cold water on Luke's high spirits.

Finally, in a matter-of-fact voice, Jeremy said: "Yeah, it's pretty interesting all right, but I think it's a tadpole that hasn't lost its tail yet."

Luke's face fell, and he muttered a small, "Oh."

Lesson 7
All About Alliteration
Composing Alliterative Sentences and Titles

Teacher Tips

This lesson is comprised of examining President John F. Kennedy's Inaugural Address with respect to alliteration, composing the analogues for 10 alliterative sentences and coming up with alliterative titles for at least four magazine articles. When they have completed the lesson, students should be adept at forming the alliterative technique.

In the culminating part of "All About Alliteration," students probably will need to do some searching on the Internet to compose their titles for the magazine articles. It is quite possible to do one or two without additional information (e.g., "Heidi Heads for Harvard" for #C. 9), but they'll need to find out more about the others.

Targeted Outcomes

- Identify alliterative passages in President Kennedy's Inaugural Address.
- Compose analogues for 10 alliterative sentences.
- Compose four alliterative magazine titles.

Name_____

All About Alliteration

**Lesson 7
Alliteration**

A. In almost all of his speeches as President, John F. Kennedy made use of a very popular literary device called alliteration. **Alliteration is the repetition of the same sound at the beginnings of words in a series**. For example, President Kennedy said this in his Inaugural Address (1961): ". . . Ask of us here the same high standards of strength and sacrifice which we ask of you . . . Let us go forth to lead the land we love, asking His blessings and His help, but knowing that here on earth God's work must be truly our own."

"Let us go forth to lead the land we love" is a prominent example of alliteration in this excerpt, but there are others. What are they?

_____

_____

B. You would be using alliteration if you said, "Mary managed to master the trick." Alliteration is especially common in titles of books and films, names of products and advertising slogans.

See if you can match each of the 10 lines that follow with an alliterative expression of your own. For example, if the first expression went "Gray and Green went go-carting in Georgia," then the second expression might be "Brown and Black boldly blasted off into space."

1. Muddy minds marvel at clarity. _____

_____

2. Sermons seldom soothe my soul. _____

_____

3. Minstrels were medieval merchants of melody, mischief and mirth. _____

_____

4. That was a terrible triumph of tomfoolery over good sense. _____

_____

5. Felines are forever fussing with their fur. _____

_____

6. Priscilla purchased a pair of pumps for the dance. _____

_____

7. In heavy traffic Howard hits his horn often. _____

_____

8. At that time in her young life, Christine crammed a lot of crusts and crumbs into her mouth. _____

_____

Name_____

All About Alliteration

**Lesson 7
Alliteration**

9. Gertrude gathered her gray coat around her shoulders and glowered at Gary. _____
_____

10. Duty required Dudley to double his efforts during December. _____
_____

C. We can often see alliteration in the names of businesses; as headings for ads; in the titles of books, articles, films and songs. Alliteration may be so common that it has lost some of its punch. See if you can use the device to come up with names for these magazine articles. Select the four that interest you most. You may have to do some research to compose your titles.

1. An article about the attempts being made to change Social Security
_____

2. An article about the dangers of Botox and other beautifying processes and products
_____

3. An article about the overuse of hype in promoting the Super Bowl
_____

4. An article about the effects of carbon dioxide gas and other air pollutants upon stratospheric ozone
_____

5. An article about the high cost of maintaining a regional symphony orchestra
_____

6. An article about education in Japan as compared with education in the United States, emphasizing the role of "cram schools" in Japan
_____

7. An article about recent developments in the music industry, especially with regard to concerts and recording
_____

8. An article about a school district that has banned the sale of soft drinks and junk food in its schools
_____

9. An article about a girl who has been admitted to Harvard University at age 12
_____

10. An article about a young man who has been arrested for entering a bank's computer files and stealing $25,000
_____

The Money-Making Mayor
Composing Alliteration Expressions

Lesson 8

Teacher Tips

By this time students should be well acquainted with alliteration and may enjoy composing their own alliterative expressions. The first part of the lesson has students supplying adjectives for a dozen given names; the second part has them incorporating three alliterations in a paragraph. There should be enough of a challenge in the tasks to occupy even the most articulate students.

Evaluating Responses

The alliterative expressions in the passage on page 25 about Gary's concerns regarding the city's politics are:

    solid, stalwart citizen

    Gary generally tried to be gracious and not to grumble

    seamy city politics

    however, he couldn't help being furious

    The mayor was making money in the most underhanded manner

    that pompous pol would plunder the city's treasury again

Lesson 8: The Money-Making Mayor
Composing Alliteration Expressions

The Lesson

These are a few of the activities that can be conducted in conjunction with this lesson:

Verbal-Linguistic Intelligence: Have students search for examples of alliteration in magazines and local newspapers.

Logical-Mathematical Intelligence: After identifying alliterative expressions in periodicals, have students determine how effective each is in its context. Does the alliteration enhance the sentence? Is the expression logical?

Interpersonal Intelligence: The class can be broken up into groups of three to compare their alliterative nicknames and decide which ones are best for each of the 12 names.

Musical-Rhythmical Intelligence: Students who enjoy rhyming might like to take one of their alliterative names and write a jingle about that personality. For example:

> Jolly, joyful Jill
> Helped us all get up the hill.
> When we said it was too high,
> She taught us how to fly!

Targeted Outcomes

- Understand and be able to use the device of alliteration.
- Compose 12 alliterative names.
- Identify three alliterative expressions in a paragraph.
- Incorporate three alliterative expressions in a paragraph about one of the nicknames in the first part of the lesson.

Name_____

The Money-Making Mayor

Nowadays sportswriters like to give players names such as "A-Rod" and "Big Hurt," but in times past, they invented nicknames such as "Splendid Splinter" (for Ted Williams, the baseball player when he was slim) and the "Galloping Ghost" (for Red Grange, who was a very elusive football halfback). Nicknames that have words that start with similar sounds are examples of alliteration. Here are some other alliterative nicknames:

Slippery Slim	Tiny Tina	Handsome Hal
Ghastly Gordon	Crafty Chris	Durable Don
Battling Bart	Terrible Tom	Vicious Vincent
Beautiful Betty	Generous Jane	Sad Sam

Would you say that Adorable Dora is also alliterative? _____

Supply these names with an alliterative adjective:

1. _____ Jamal   5. _____ David   9. _____ Maria
2. _____ Tiffany 6. _____ Susan 10. _____ Kelly
3. _____ Kaitlin 7. _____ Pepe   11. _____ Justin
4. _____ Becky   8. _____ Lindsay 12. _____ Sal

Underline the alliterative expressions in this paragraph.

Since he was always regarded as a solid, stalwart citizen, Gary generally tried to be gracious and not to grumble about the seamy city politics. On this occasion, however, he couldn't help being furious. The mayor was making money in the most underhanded manner. Gary didn't want to precipitate a crisis, but this time he had to blow the whistle or that pompous pol would plunder the city's treasury again.

Select one of your alliterative names and write a paragraph about that person. Include three alliterative expressions in your paragraph.

_____

_____

_____

_____

_____

_____

Hink-Pinks
Producing Rhymed Pairs of Words

Lesson 9

Teacher Tips

The game of hink-pink (or hinky-pinky for words with two syllables) is well known. Its continuing popularity may be due to an inexhaustible number of rhyming words that can be used in the game to stimulate the minds of young and old. Hink-pink is included in this book because young people continue to enjoy rhyme.

Our contribution to the game is to introduce the element of adding a rhyme to tell a story. Encourage students to play this variation of the game, which is more challenging than the original.

Evaluating Responses

The following are acceptable answers to the dozen think links on page 27:

1. obese feline = fat cat
2. unfair hit = low blow
3. ruddy cranium = red head
4. correct evening = right night
5. moist vagrant = damp tramp
6. plain-spoken shorty = blunt runt
7. brilliant luminescence = bright light
8. tardy spouse = late mate
9. tidy Peter = neat Pete
10. lean epidermis = thin skin
11. bashful boy = shy guy
12. negligible altercation = slight fight

Targeted Outcomes

- Produce rhymed pairs of words for the 12 definitions given.
- Compose a series of three rhymed pairs that tell a brief story.

Name_____

Hink-Pinks

Lesson 9
Rhyme

A. A hink-pink is a pair of one-syllable words that's defined by a given phrase. To form a hink-pink, study the clue phrase and think of two rhyming words that are synonyms for the words in the phrase. For example, when given the expression "pleased father," you might think of "glad dad." Think of a pair of rhyming words for these sets of words. Each word should be one syllable. You can use a dictionary or thesaurus if you get stuck.

1. obese feline _____
2. unfair hit _____
3. ruddy cranium _____
4. correct evening _____
5. moist vagrant _____
6. plain-spoken shorty _____
7. brilliant luminescence _____
8. tardy spouse _____
9. tidy Peter _____
10. lean epidermis _____
11. bashful boy _____
12. negligible altercation _____

Think of another set of words in which one rhymed pair is about equal to another.

_____

B. Maybe you can think of a series of rhymed pairs that tells a little story, as in "no dough = no go = no show."

_____

_____

_____

Lesson 10

Wise 'n' Rhymers
Providing New Rhyming Endings for Old Sayings

Teacher Tips

Since it takes time to think of new endings for the 10 sayings, this lesson consists of only one activity. Although the rhyming should appeal to students, it isn't always easy to make the new endings rhyme. For instance, an ironic ending to "A fool and his gold are soon parted" might be "A fool and his gold were lucky to get together in the first place." That doesn't rhyme and won't do.

It's possible that your students will want to share their sayings with each other. Although this activity doesn't result in genuine literary merit, one or two gems just might be produced.

Evaluating Responses

These are possible rhyming endings to the 10 sayings on page 29. A number of other responses may do as well or better.

1. If at first you don't succeed, to a higher power you should plead.
2. When the cat's away, it's a better day.
3. Water and oil, and the car won't boil.
4. You can't tell a book by its look.
5. A fool and his gold are soon rolled.
6. He who fights and runs away learns it's not really okay.
7. Look before you cook.
8. That's a nice bowl of rice!
9. Sticks and stones may break my bones, but names will provoke no groans or moans.
10. There's many a slip 'twixt the bill and the tip.

Follow Through

If your students have little trouble composing the endings, you can have them find other sayings that can be humorously changed. Reference books such as *Bartlett's Familiar Quotations* could be helpful. If during the course of this lesson a few genuinely humorous sayings are produced, they can be included in a student publication.

Targeted Outcomes

- Invent new endings that rhyme for 10 well-known sayings.

Reference: Bartlett, John. *Bartlett's Familiar Quotations*. New York: Little, Brown and Company, 2002.

Name_____

Wise 'n' Rhymers

Lesson 10

It can be amusing to take an old saying and alter it, making it either funny or ironic. For example, take the familiar saying about handling pressure and change it like this:

If you can't stand the heat, find another seat.

Or the one about self-pity:

Laugh and the world laughs with you, cry and you'll go "boo-hoo."

Change these old sayings into new ones. Cross out the second line and write your new line next to it. Try to make your saying rhyme.

1. If at first you don't succeed,

   try, try again. _____

2. When the cat's away,

   the mice will play. _____

3. Oil and water

   don't mix. _____

4. You can't tell a book

   by its cover. _____

5. A fool and his gold

   are soon parted. _____

6. He who fights and runs away

   lives to fight another day. _____

7. Look before

   you leap. _____

8. That's a nice

   kettle of fish! _____

9. Sticks and stones may break my bones,

   but names will never hurt me. _____

10. There's many a slip

    'twixt the cup and the lip. _____

Lesson 11

Quick Milk
Solving Riddles

Teacher Tips

Riddles tend to be popular with young children, but older kids enjoy them too. Three of the four riddles featured in this activity on page 31 are mostly old ones, but it's doubtful if students have encountered the last one.

Probably the most interesting part of the activity is the invitation to create some good riddles. This may trigger a riddling session, a pleasant and welcome break from the routine.

Evaluating Responses

As Mario demonstrated with his answer about a door that isn't a door, there can be more than one answer to a riddle. Nevertheless, here are the answers to the four riddles:

Milk is quick because it's pasteurized (past yer eyes) before you see it! This is a good example of the use of a pun in a riddle. A high percentage of riddles are puns.

A door isn't a door when it's ajar.

At the North Pole any way you go is south.

A shadow becomes darker when it (the daylight) becomes lighter. Some eyeglasses get darker in brighter light, also.

Targeted Outcomes

- Recognize the use of the pun in riddles.
- Write three or more riddles with puns.

Name_____

Quick Milk

Mario laughed and laughed.

But his friend Abe just looked puzzled. Mario had just asked Abe, "Why is milk so quick?" When Abe couldn't answer, Mario almost fell over because he laughed so hard. Although it was an old riddle, Abe hadn't heard it before and couldn't understand why milk was "quick."

"Oh, maybe," he thought, "when I'm very thirsty and drink it in a hurry." But he didn't say that to Mario.

What is the answer to the riddle? _____

Abe got even, though, because he thought of a riddle that his mother had told him a few weeks ago. "Okay, if you're so smart, Mario, when is a door not a door?"

Mario stopped laughing and frowned. He couldn't think of how a door couldn't be a door. Finally he replied, "When it's a window."

"Why do you say that?" asked Abe.

"I guess because I've read about people using French windows as doors," said Mario.

Maybe he was right. What is the usual answer? _____

Mr. Harding, their teacher, had overheard the conversation and interrupted. "I've got a couple of riddles for you two," he said. "See if you can answer these. Where will you always travel south, no matter which way you are headed?"

"Oh, I think I know that one," said Abe. And he did. What is the answer? _____

"Okay," said Mr. Harding. "Now what becomes darker during the day, when it's lighter?"

Both boys were stumped. They came up with answers about food, computers, clothing and clouds, but they

didn't have a good answer. Do you? _____ What is it? _____

What are a few of your favorite riddles? _____

_____

_____

_____

_____

_____

Lesson 12

The Paws That Refreshes

Inventing Punny Names for Animals
Matching Names with Animals
Drawing an Animal with a Punny Name

Teacher Tips

This is a lighthearted lesson. It deals in puns and drawing. That doesn't mean that students won't have to think, however. They will have to invent punny names, and that can be difficult. The emphasis will be on originality and humor. In order for students to be both playful and original, warm them up with a few puns.

Select a few headlines from the newspaper. You could find "Copy Cat" (about the first kitten to be cloned) or "Knights Slay Dragons" (a basketball team whose nickname is "Knights" beats one which is nicknamed "Dragons"). You might also ask students what a "seal of approval" looks like. Is it a seal that smiles?

Students should have little difficulty in determining which animals go with the dozen names on page 34 concocted by the Humane Society, until they reach the last two. Those two names might have been given to several animals. Here are the obvious answers to the first 10:

1. Clint Eastwoof—a dog
2. The Great Catsby—a cat
3. Elvis Purrsly—a cat
4. Napoleon Bone-Apart—a dog
5. Jane Hounda—a dog
6. Carol Purrnet—a cat
7. Winston Church-hare—a rabbit
8. Kitty-Patra—a cat
9. Drew Burybone—a dog
10. Bark Antony—a dog

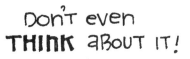

The Paws That Refreshes

Inventing Punny Names for Animals
Matching Names with Animals
Drawing an Animal with a Punny Name

Lesson 12

Ronald Reekin (#A. 11) could be a skunk or a weasel. All of the members of the weasel family are capable of creating unpleasant odors. In addition to the skunk, the weasel family includes the badger, marten, ferret, ermine, otter and wolverine. Pokey Roberts (#A. 12) could be turtle, tortoise, sloth, snail or slug.

Drawing a picture of one of the animals should appeal to students, especially those who are talented in creating cartoons, sketches or portraits. You may choose to have those students who aren't artistic to copy from photographs found in reference books or in the comic section of the newspaper.

Punning comes very naturally to some people, but can be difficult or distasteful to others. A glance at any newspaper, especially its sports section, will confirm punning is not a forgotten art. Coming up with three more famous names that can be made into puns about animals will probably be a challenging task for many students. Try it yourself. It isn't too hard to come up with "Meryl Sheep," "Mohammed Alleycat" or "Lucille Bull."

Targeted Outcomes

- Recognize the humor in puns.
- Invent three puns, using the names of famous people for animals.

Name_____ **Lesson 12**
The Paws That Refreshes *Puns*

A. The Humane Society of a county in the West tried to instigate the adoption of some animals needing a home with a full-page advertisement in the local newspaper. Each caption was accompanied by a clever description of the animal and its photograph. As you can quickly see by scanning the assigned names for the animals, the people at the Humane Society used puns to try to capture the attention of potential adopters. What animal goes with each name?

1. Clint Eastwoof _____

2. The Great Catsby _____

3. Elvis Purrsly _____

4. Napoleon Bone-Apart _____

5. Jane Hounda _____

6. Carol Purrnet _____

7. Winston Church-Hare _____

8. Kitty-Patra _____

9. Drew Burybone _____

10. Bark Antony _____

11. Ronald Reekin _____

12. Pokey Roberts _____

Name_____ **Lesson 12**
The Paws That Refreshes *Puns*

B. Draw a picture of one of the animals the Humane Society was putting up for adoption.

C. Can you come up with three other punny names for animals? You needn't restrict yourself to dogs and cats. There have been some funny names given to animal characters in cartoons, such as skunks, coyotes, bears, wolves, pigs, birds and foxes. These animals and others can be given punny names. For instance, you might think of "Davy Croakit" for a frog or "Mary Tyler Moo-er" for a cow. Try to invent at least three names.

1. _____

2. _____

3. _____

4. _____

5. _____

Lesson 13

But Who's the Father?
Identifying Personification in Maxims

Teacher Tips

This lesson about personification also features the maxim. There is very little difference between maxims and adages or aphorisms, but, in general, maxims offer advice. In the second part of the lesson students are asked if any of the maxims offer questionable advice. Some may wonder if "opportunity" really only knocks once or if "virtue's" comrade is "good fortune" (are virtuous people always lucky?).

Evaluating Responses

Of the 10 sayings on page 37, four are definitely legitimate examples of personification and two are debatable.

1. "Two heads are better than one" has no personification (but it is a good example of synecdoche).
2. "Brevity is the soul of wit" has personification because it equates the abstraction with soul.
3. "Good fortune is the comrade of virtue" is a clear-cut example of personification, treating "good fortune" as a comrade or companion.
4. "Opportunity only knocks once—don't dally" has "opportunity" knocking at a door and so is a fine example of personification.
5. "Two many cooks spoil the broth" has no personification.
6. "Don't put all of your eggs in one basket" is just straightforward advice.
7. "Too much arguing makes truth go astray" is an example of personification because "truth" is being treated as if it were a person who is caused to go astray.
8. "Haste makes waste" almost qualifies as personification. A case might be made that "haste" is making waste, as a person could, but it's not a clear example of personification.
9. "Elbow grease gives the best polish" is also close to being an example of personification because "elbow grease" gives the polish.
10. "We never miss the water until the well goes dry" is a sage comment and a warning, but it has no personification.

Targeted Outcomes

- Learn what personification is.
- Learn what a maxim is.
- Identify the four examples of personification in 10 maxims.

Name_____

Lesson 13
Personification, Maxims

But Who's the Father?

A. If you have ever said "Necessity is the mother of invention," you have used a figure of speech called personification. **Personification is a way of speaking or writing in which an inanimate object or abstraction is given human qualities.** When you take a word such as *necessity* and talk as if it were a person, you are using personification. "Slowly climb the moon-touched mountains up their stairway to the sky" is also an example—although a fancy one—of personification.

A maxim is a succinct saying that expresses a general truth or a rule of conduct. Which of these maxims have true personification? Underline the sayings that do.

1. Two heads are better than one.
2. Brevity is the soul of wit.
3. Good fortune is the comrade of virtue.
4. Opportunity only knocks once—don't dally.
5. Too many cooks spoil the broth.
6. Don't put all of your eggs in one basket.
7. Too much arguing makes truth go astray.
8. Haste makes waste.
9. Elbow grease gives the best polish.
10. We never miss the water until the well goes dry.

B. Look over those sayings again. Which one seems to be particularly wise to you?

_____

Why does it seem so? _____

_____

Do you consider one of them rather doubtful? _____

Why do you feel that way? _____

_____

Lesson 14
Some Persons Who Aren't
Writing a Verse Based on a Personification

Teacher Tips

This lesson deals with one of the most important literary devices—personification. It's comprised of two quotations, some examples and an invitation to write a quatrain. Many students may prefer to use a rhyme scheme such as aabb, abaca, or abab; but it will also be easy for some to write in free verse. The verse about hope on page 39 can serve as a model. You may want to add one or more meaningful items to the seven personifications suggested.

Evaluating Responses

Students are asked to select a personification that interests them and then compose a quatrain based on it. For students who choose to write their poem in free verse, you might review the features of that form—it is verse without a metrical pattern, and its lines are divided according to cadences or natural patterns of speech.

William Blake's quatrain in his "Auguries of Innocence" can serve as a model for verse that has a metrical pattern:

> To see a world in a grain of sand,
> And a heaven in a wild flower;
> Hold infinity in the palm of your hand,
> And eternity in an hour.

Targeted Outcomes

- Learn the definition of *personification*.
- Write a quatrain based on a personification.

Name_____

Lesson 14
Personification

Some Persons Who Aren't

In Stephen Crane's short story, "The Open Boat," the author wrote that "[Nature] did not seem cruel to him then, nor beneficent, nor treacherous, nor wise." Crane endows Nature with human attributes, rather like a mysterious personality. This way of writing (and thinking) is called personifying a non-human thing. **Personification is a figure of speech that gives animals, objects and ideas human characteristics.**

Writers are fond of making personalities of inanimate things such as mountains, rivers, boats, ships, automobiles, guns, shoes and storms. They also give human characteristics to ideas such as fate, death, luck, justice, liberty, beauty and hope. This is one writer's attempt to personify hope:

> Frail gray friend
> Where's your rosy flow?
> Each day you grow more fragile,
> Less a reality, more a ghost.
> —Are you Hope?

Personification is one of the most popular rhetorical devices in literature and is often found in poetry. Take one of these personifications and write a quatrain (a four-line stanza) about one that especially interests you. Your verse doesn't have to rhyme, but you may find it easier to write if you rhyme at least two lines.

- time as an overpowering adversary
- a bicycle as a loyal friend
- spring as a lovely girl
- a mountain as a brooding giant
- a jalopy as a disreputable man
- a cake as a beckoning temptress
- pain as a constant companion

Which personification interests you most? _____

To get started, write the thoughts that come into your mind when you think of that subject. Then write a quatrain.

_____

_____

_____

_____

_____

_____

_____

_____

Lesson 15

Losing in Order to Win
Thinking about Paradoxes
Writing a Personal Anecdote

Teacher Tips

Using this lesson, we try to strike some responsible chords in the subconsciousness of students. As is the case with many of the lessons in this book, there are no right or wrong answers. Students should try not to miss the mark in figuring out the paradoxical expressions. Therefore, the lead-in or warm-up is critical to the success of the lesson.

There are many examples of the idea that in order to win one must first lose. The baseball example on page 42 is in the introductory section. You might discuss this kind of paradox by mentioning one or two other examples. Although students should give purely personal reactions to the paradoxes, you should make sure that they have grasped the idea; thus a discussion before the lesson is necessary.

"Losing in Order to Win" is intended to be a challenging exercise. In order to respond adequately, students will have to do some thinking. There may be a few who will quickly become frustrated or discouraged, but all of the paradoxes can be interpreted by middle-school students. For instance, the paradox about hurrying to take it easy should be familiar to them. Most of us rush to complete a task in order to relax later on.

Evaluating Responses

1. **Hurrying in order to take it easy**
   People frequently hurry to complete a task in order to be free to relax, go on vacation and so on.

2. **Becoming invisible in order to become apparent**
   Sometimes when you are missing from a group that you are usually a part of, your absence is noted more than your presence would have been.

3. **Crying that produces laughter**
   After a good cry, we can often laugh at ourselves. Also, a comedian can cry in such an absurd way that it evokes laughter.

4. **Laughter that results in crying**
   Some people laugh so much that tears come to their eyes. Laughter can also be cruel and cause tears in the one who is ridiculed.

5. **Starving in order to eat**
   Many people go on a diet, almost starving themselves, with the goal in mind of having a huge and rich dessert at the end of the diet.

Lesson 15

Losing in Order to Win
Thinking About Paradoxes
Writing a Personal Anecdote

6. Eating in order to starve

Foods with "empty calories" don't actually starve you, but they deprive you of vitamins and nutrients and may starve some tissues. Junk food addicts are therefore eating to starve themselves in this way.

7. Closing your eyes in order to see

People will often shut their eyes in order to block out the images before them so that they can visualize (in their minds) a particular face or scene.

8. Appearing in order to be invisible

There is such a thing as "hiding in a crowd." You are visible, but you can't be distinguished from the others.

The Writing Assignment

Although students need to imagine situations to fit the paradoxes, they are not being asked to come up with plots, choose one and then expand it into a short story. However, if the lesson is successful, and the timing is right, you might want to have them do that. The idea is to encourage students to think and write individual perspectives. Therefore, students are asked to write about a paradox that has had, or might have, a bearing on them personally.

Students' writing will be mainly anecdotal. Those who have a talent for arranging words in varying patterns and sequences will probably find an interesting way to organize their remarks. The writing itself shouldn't have any unnecessary requirements; there should be no real concern about form—except that the remarks should be in paragraphs.

Targeted Outcomes

- Gain a better understanding of the paradox.
- Explain eight paradoxes.
- Think of one or more paradoxes.
- Write a personal anecdote based on a paradox.

Name_____

Lesson 15
Paradoxes, Anecdotes

Losing in Order to Win

A. During the strike-blighted 1981 major league baseball season, there was a brouhaha about the possibility of teams "throwing" games in order to ensure their winning a favorable playoff spot. It was feared that in order to meet a weaker team in the playoffs, strong teams would deliberately lose games and thereby be pitted against inferior teams rather than superior ones. In this way, they might "win by losing." This kind of a situation is called a paradox. A paradox occurs when two seemingly contradictory possibilities share some plausible relationship. Something in the situation or in the characters involved in the events is seemingly inconsistent and yet proves reasonable.

As odd as it may seem, there have been many occasions when people realized that they could win by losing. Can you think of a situation where a person could lose by winning? Describe it.

_____
_____
_____
_____

B. Here are more paradoxes. Explain how each one can make sense.

1. Hurrying in order to take it easy _____
_____
_____
_____

2. Becoming invisible in order to become apparent _____
_____
_____
_____

3. Crying that produces laughter _____
_____
_____
_____

4. Laughter that results in crying _____
_____
_____

Name _____

Losing in Order to Win

Lesson 15
Paradoxes, Anecdotes

5. Starving in order to eat _____
   _____
   _____
   _____

6. Eating in order to starve _____
   _____
   _____
   _____

7. Closing your eyes in order to see _____
   _____
   _____
   _____

8. Appearing in order to be invisible _____
   _____
   _____
   _____

C. Choose one of the previous paradoxes—or any other one you prefer—and tell how it could have, or has had, a bearing on your life.
   _____
   _____
   _____
   _____
   _____
   _____

Lesson 16

Make Mine Candy
Examining Irony
Writing an Ironic Cinquain

Teacher Tips

As Adelstein and Pival (1967) point out in *The Writing Commitment,* irony is achieved by incongruity—a pairing of opposites or perspectives, one of which may mask or reveal the real truth. Closely related to sarcasm, irony can be achieved through understatement or exaggeration. Sarcasm is harsher, as when one ball player says to another—"Nice going!"—after the teammate has muffed a grounder badly. The tone of irony, in contrast, is wryly humorous.

The cinquain on page 45 presented as an example in this lesson satisfies the requirements of the two forms that the verse has been given. It has a 2-4-6-8-2 syllabic pattern as well as the 1-2-3-4-1 word pattern that many teachers prefer.

Targeted Outcomes

• Gain a better understanding of irony.
• Write an ironic cinquain.

Reference: Adelstein, M.E., and J.G. Pival. *The Writing Commitment.* New York: Harcourt Brace Jovanovich, 1967.

Name_____

Make Mine Candy

One way of achieving humor or putting over a point is to use irony. Irony implies that there is something very different from what is said or written. In verbal irony the speaker or writer deliberately expresses an idea so that it can be understood in two ways; it forces the listener or reader to find the true meaning. Here's a sampling of ironic statements:

> He had occasional flashes of silence that made his conversation perfectly delightful.
>
> It's no trick to quit smoking—I've done it dozens of times. (Attributed to Mark Twain)
>
> I married beneath me. All women do. (Nancy Astor)
>
> Nobody shoots at Santa Claus. (Al Smith)

Irony can be achieved by a surprise or a twist, as illustrated by this cinquain:

> Candy
>
> Yummy, scrumptious
>
> Munching, crunching, snacking
>
> Always satisfies my craving—
>
> Pimples.

Write a cinquain that has a twist or surprise ending. The cinquain follows this pattern:

> First line—one word, giving the title
>
> Second line—two words, describing the title
>
> Third line—three words, expressing an action
>
> Fourth line—four words, expressing a feeling
>
> Fifth line—another word for the title

_____

_____

_____

_____

_____

Lesson 17

Whistling Cops
Explaining the Similarities Between Seven Pairs of Things
Writing a Character Sketch That Has at Least One Analogy

Teacher Tips

This is a challenging lesson. A definition of an *analogy* is given following an example of a literary analogy. Students are to point out similarities between seven sets of disparate things (traffic cop and tea kettle, miner and gopher, and the like) and then think of two or more similarities for each. Lastly, they are asked to write a character sketch. Adequate time should be allowed for students to develop the sketch properly.

Evaluating Responses

These are some possible responses to the seven prompts on page 47. Students may come up with better ones.

1. traffic cop and tea kettle—They both can whistle and they both may have brass.
2. miner and gopher—They dig in the ground, and they live in tunnels.
3. baseball outfielder and frog—They both catch flies, and at times must move quickly to do their catching after being relatively stationary.
4. gossip columnist and seagull—They pick up bits of things (gossipy conversation and food), and they are always on the alert for new developments.
5. airline pilot and elevator—They keep going up and down, and they carry passengers.
6. magazine salesperson and dollar bill—They both go from person to person, and sooner or later they get worn out.
7. lion tamer and musician—They must pay close attention to what they are doing and must possess a certain amount of natural talent.

Targeted Outcomes

- Learn the nature of analogy.
- Explain the similarities between seven pairs of things.
- Write a character sketch that has at least one analogy.

Name_____

Whistling Cops

Lesson 17
*Analogy,
Character Sketch*

A. Receiving congratulations is like taking a warm bath. After a genuinely good performance, we anticipate approval in the same way we look forward to a nice, warm bath after exerting ourselves in a worthwhile physical endeavor. The bath envelopes us, as do the welcome words of our admirers. We bathe luxuriously as a rewarding comfort. We know that the glow won't last forever—but we are grateful for the exultant feeling.

The name for this way of comparing things is analogy. **An analogy, like a simile or metaphor, compares things that are not usually seen as being similar**. Unlike them, however, an analogy often notes several points of similarity and not only one.

B. Here are eight pairs of dissimilar things. Give at least two reasons why the paired things can be comparable. For example, if you were given the pair of a lie and fog, you could point out that both of them can conceal things and also that they both can distort the way we see things.

1. How are a traffic cop and a tea kettle alike? _____
   _____

2. Why is a miner like a gopher? _____
   _____

3. How are a baseball outfielder and a frog alike?_____
   _____

4. How is a gossip columnist like a sea gull? _____
   _____

5. Why is an airline pilot like an elevator?_____
   _____

6. How are a magazine salesperson and a dollar bill alike? _____
   _____

7. Why is a lion tamer like a musician? _____
   _____

Name_____

Whistling Cops

Lesson 17
Analogy, Character Sketch

C. Now incorporate one or more analogies in a character sketch to make it more vivid and enjoyable.

A character sketch is a literary portrait of a person; it outlines the main personality traits of the person. The primary purpose of a character sketch is to inform, but it can also impress or entertain the reader or praise the subject. In writing a character sketch, select someone you know quite well as the subject; that person should also be interesting to your readers. The facts, traits, idiosyncrasies and accomplishments of the subject provide the fabric of the character sketch. Anecdotes and quotes are also helpful in portraying the subject. You can stress the subject's personality, appearance, character or accomplishments.

A character sketch has an introduction, middle section and close. The introduction contains one or two of the most important traits of the subject. The middle section contains more details and also provides a revealing glimpse of the subject. The close summarizes the subject's personality or character.

Examine your first draft with a critical eye. Look closely to see if your sketch gives the reader a clear picture of your subject. It helps a great deal to have another person read your second draft in an objective way. Listen carefully to any suggestions. Ask yourself if you are satisfied with the final draft.

Apt Comparisons
Composing Analogies

Lesson 18

Teacher Tips

There are a number of definitions given in this lesson, among them the simile and the metaphor, therefore "Apt Comparisons" can serve as a review of lessons. Students are to identify the analogy in a paragraph and compose analogies for seven pairs of things.

Evaluating Responses

In the paragraph on page 50, hikers stranded on the side of a mountain trying to keep from freezing are compared with a hive of bees that have balled up to retain enough heat to stay alive. (We expect the bees to be successful—no telling about the freezing hikers.)

Students may see other points of similarity between the pairs of things to analogize, but these are some obvious ones:

1. a snake and a river—winding
2. ants and motorists—following pathways
3. butterflies and young women—they often flit around; they metamorphosize
4. chipmunks and kindergartners—they scramble around
5. a talkative person and a faucet—once turned on, they keep pouring forth
6. clouds and lies—they come apart easily
7. a coach and an alpha male wolf—they growl and glower at players who don't perform properly.

Check periodically to see that students have written analogies and not similes or metaphors.

Targeted Outcomes

- Learn the definition of an analogy,
- Identify the analogy in a paragraph about hikers huddled on the side of a mountain.
- Compose analogies for seven pairs of things.

Name_____

Lesson 18
Analogies

Apt Comparisons

The tall shortstop, in the manner of a crane stabbing at a minnow and coming up with an empty bill, fumbled the ball between his legs and then stared at his offending glove.

In the sentence above a comparison is made between a gawky ball player and a long-legged bird. The purpose of comparing such dissimilar creatures is to create an image in the mind of the reader of long-legged ineptitude. This type of comparison is called a **literary analogy—the showing of one or more similarities between two things that are not ordinarily considered similar**. In pointing out a likeness between two things, a writer is able to enrich the imagery of the prose or poetry and also to increase the reader's understanding of what is depicted or discussed.

What is the analogy in the following paragraph? When you have identified it, write the two things that are being compared and the characteristic they share.

> It was exceptionally cold that night on the side of the mountain. Although the blizzard had subsided, the hikers were just slightly relieved because the crevice only partially shielded them from the icy winds that whipped around the rocks. Their only salvation was the fact that there were four of them, not anywhere near the number of bees in a hive who cling together to preserve and conserve life-sustaining heat during a cold spell, yet enough to keep each other warm—and alive—in a common embrace.

_____

_____

_____

_____

Similes, metaphors and analogies all make comparisons. Following are examples of each figure of speech:

> Justin simply sat there like a punctured balloon when he heard that he wasn't chosen to represent his school at the convention.

"Like a punctured balloon" is a simile. **A simile specifies a likeness** and uses the words *like* and *as*. Justin is being compared to a punctured balloon.

> The principal's announcement took all the wind out of Justin's sails when he learned that he wasn't chosen to represent his school at the convention.

A metaphor states that something is something else, thereby implying a likeness. In the example above, the announcement took the wind from Justin's sails, but of course Justin is not a sailboat. This expression is also an **idiom, a common saying that has an unusual construction** ("turned him in" for "informed on him") **or that is not literally true** ("stirred up a hornets' nest" for "created a controversy").

> His ego utterly deflated, Justin sat rigidly in his seat. Ideas of being greatly admired by his classmates and regarded as one of the outstanding students of the state had filled his head. These thoughts inflated his ego in the same way that air inflates a balloon. The trouble with a balloon that has been stretched tightly by air is that just the slightest contact with a sharp object will pop it. So it was with Justin when he heard the principal's announcement on the intercom. It was the awful pricking of his ego-balloon.

Name_____

Apt Comparisons

Justin's ego and a tight balloon are compared in the preceding analogy on page 50. The analogy is a simple one that is emphasized by the last word, *ego-balloon*. In an extended analogy, several points of comparison are made. Some writers devote several paragraphs when making that kind of analogy.

Write analogies to compare between these things:

1. a snake and a river _____
_____

2. ants and motorists _____
_____

3. butterflies and young women _____
_____

4. chipmunks and kindergartners _____
_____

5. a talkative person and a faucet _____
_____

6. clouds and lies _____
_____

7. a coach and an alpha male wolf _____
_____

TLC10563 Copyright © Teaching & Learning Company, Carthage, IL 62321-0010

Lesson 19: The Handsome Stranger
Hyperbole

Teacher Tips

Most of us exaggerate from time to time in order to emphasize a point or as a consequence of natural exuberance. When exaggeration is used deliberately in writing, it's done to create an effect upon the reader. This lesson offers two examples of hyperbole, the first is typical of the way many young people talk. The second is an exaggeration concocted by writers who want to be humorous.

Present this lesson as a warm-up before giving students "Tall Tales" (Lesson 20).

Evaluating Responses

Lola exaggerates in the following parts of her narration on page 53:

> ". . . very gorgeous brown cowboy outfit that must have cost thousands and thousands of dollars."

> ". . . this town that had the ugliest, nastiest men you've ever seen."

> "His smile was so sneaky and awful it could have curdled milk at 20 paces."

> "She had on a sensational blue dress with a million shiny spangles on it."

The author includes these exaggerations from the story on page 54:

> "She sang as she came to breakfast, and the milk curdled."

> " . . . and the bristles fell out of the toothbrush."

> "Two birds fell from the trees, never to twitter and fly again."

Targeted Outcomes

- Learn the uses of hyperbole as a figure of speech in writing.
- Identify three instances of exaggeration in a young girl's speech.
- Identify two instances of hyperbole in the story about Matilda.

The Handsome Stranger

Lesson 19
Hyperbole

A. **Hyperbole, or exaggeration, is a figure of speech used to emphasize a point, an opinion or a situation.** It is found in the speech of most young people—and a few old-timers too. Here are some examples of hyperbole:

- I was so tired I could have slept a year.
- His arm was bigger around than a grown man's waist.
- That book weighs a ton.
- We are all big huggers in these parts, and once we get a regular natural embrace it takes us a day to get apart.
- One day it was really cold—about three hundred and eighty below zero.

B. The following is a father's account of his daughter's obsession with television. In his daughter's narration, there are several instances when she exaggerated. Read the passage once, then read it again underlining the places where she exaggerated.

Lola was a great television viewer. When she was only a toddler Lola would toddle to the living room and switch on the TV. Because this usually happened at 5:45 a.m., nothing much would appear on the screen from her favorite channel, but Lola would continually stare at the screen until something happened in TV Land. As she grew older, Lola's enthusiasm for the programs she watched prompted her to give accounts to her family of the dramas and comedies that she had seen. It should be added that Lola had a lively imagination.

One evening at dinner Lola bounced onto her seat next to her older brother and commenced to give a detailed account of a western she had just watched:

"That was the most fabulous program I've ever seen! There's this handsome guy in a very gorgeous brown cowboy outfit that must have cost thousands and thousands of dollars. He came into this town that had the ugliest, nastiest men you've ever seen. When he entered a room, every face in the place turned toward him, and you just knew there would be a fight because one of them belonged to this beautiful blonde girl and she was sitting at a table next to this guy with a tiny moustache and a scar on his cheek.

"The handsome guy was looking for his brother, but the wimp of a waiter wouldn't give him any information at all. The waiter kept glancing at the guy with the scar on his cheek and he would smile. His smile was so sneaky and awful it could have curdled milk at 20 paces, but I didn't see anyone drinking milk. The handsome guy casually turned to look where the waiter was glancing. When he did, he didn't pay much attention to Scarface, but he noticed the beautiful blonde all right. She had on a sensational blue dress with a million shiny spangles on it . . ."

Twenty-five minutes later—after dessert—Lola got to the fight.

Name_____

Lesson 19
Hyperbole
The Handsome Stranger

C. For hyperbole to be effective in writing, it must not be overdone. If you exaggerate, don't go too far. Hyperbole is often one of the main ingredients in humorous writing, but the writer must take care to make the exaggerations almost believable. Following is an example:

Songbird

Matilda Tibbetts wanted to be a famous singer. From the time she was a little girl she imagined herself singing in theaters and auditoriums all over the world. She just knew she would become a marvelous singer. Since her parents wanted to be kind, they didn't tell Matilda that she had one of the worse singing voices they had ever heard. It turned out that Matilda was tone deaf.

As she grew older, Matilda began to sing more often. She sang as she came to breakfast, and the milk curdled. She sang before she brushed her teeth, and the bristles fell out of the toothbrush. She sang to her dolls, she sang to her mirror and she sang to her dog. The dog always howled and ran away when she did that. One day, Matilda heard the birds singing outside. She ran out and tried to sing with them. Two birds fell from the trees, never to twitter and fly again.

Finally, after an eventful girlhood, Matilda met someone who didn't want to leave suddenly when she began to sing. In a short time they were engaged. Later, when they were married, she sang every day in the kitchen. Although they had to buy a lot of milk, they were happy. Her husband admired Matilda a lot. Of course, he was tone deaf too.

Now read the passage again and underline the parts where the author exaggerated.

Tall Tales
Writing a Tall Tale

Lesson 20

Teacher Tips

Hyperbole, or exaggeration, as a figure of speech is not used to deceive but to emphasize a statement or situation. Exaggeration is a popular technique for infusing humor into a piece of writing (Erma Bombeck was especially adept at it in her newspaper columns), but it is not surefire by any means. Inexperienced writers tend to overdo their exaggerated statements and quotations, resulting in pieces that are not really funny.

Tall tales, on the other hand, are dependent upon hyperbole, as the well-known story about Kit Carson on page 56 demonstrates. It is therefore much safer for students to write tall tales than it is for them to write humorous pieces that feature hyperbole.

Evaluating Responses

It is extremely difficult for students to avoid seizing on the themes of violence, strength and derring-do that young people are continually exposed to. The seven topics presented on page 57 have themes of generosity, hospitality and selfishness.

It is suggested that you look at students' tall tales somewhat differently from their other writings. Characterization, for instance, will probably take care of itself. Warn them to keep exaggerations within the bounds of the "improbable but vaguely possible" and in good taste.

Targeted Outcomes

- Compose hyperbolic statements for seven topics.
- Write a tall tale based on one of those statements.

Name_____

Tall Tales

Lesson 20
Hyperbole

You may have heard the tall tale about Kit Carson and the famous echo in Wyoming. It was said that in the Valley of Echoes in Jackson County it took eight hours for an echo to return. If a cowboy shouted "It's time to get up" as he went to bed, the echo would wake him up in the morning.

That tale is humorous because it's an example of fanciful exaggeration or hyperbole. Its humor is found in its outrageousness. In tall tales such as this there is no pretending that statements are believable—they are obviously preposterous. But they are fun to hear and to read.

Here is a second tall tale about another legendary folk hero, Pecos Bill:

> According to the most veracious historians, Bill was born about the time Sam Houston discovered Texas. He cut his teeth on a Bowie knife, and his earliest playfellows were the bears and catamounts of east Texas.
>
> When Bill was about a year old, another family moved into the county and settled about fifty miles down the river. His father decided the place was getting too crowded, and so he packed his family in a wagon and headed west.
>
> One day after they had crossed the Pecos River, Bill fell out of the wagon. As there were sixteen or seventeen other children in the family, his parents didn't miss him for four or five weeks, and then it was too late to try to find him.
>
> That's how Bill came to grow up with the coyotes along the Pecos. He soon learned the coyote language, and he used to hunt with them and sit on the hills and howl at night. Being so young when he got lost, he always thought he was a coyote. That's where he learned to kill deer by running them to death.
>
> One day when he was about ten years old a cowboy came along just when Bill had matched a fight with two grizzly bears. Bill hugged the bears to death, tore off a hind leg of one, and was just settin' down to breakfast when this cowboy loped up and asked him what he meant by runnin' around naked that way with the varmints.
>
> "Why, because I am a varmint," Bill told him. "I'm a coyote."
>
> The cowboy argued with him that he was a human, but Bill wouldn't believe him.
>
> "Ain't I got fleas?" he insisted. "And don't I howl around all night, like a respectable coyote should do?"
>
> "That don't prove nothin'," the cowboy answered. "All Texans have fleas, and most of them howl. Did you ever see a coyote that didn't have a tail? Well, you ain't got no tail; so that proves you ain't a varmint."
>
> Bill looked, and, sure enough, he didn't have a tail.
>
> "You sure got me out on a limb," says Bill. "I never noticed that before. It shows what higher education will do for a man. I believe you're right. Lead me to them humans, and I'll throw in with them."

Name _____

Tall Tales

Lesson 20
Hyperbole

Write an exaggerated statement about each of the following topics:

1. The kindness of a certain woman _____

_____

2. The food served at a cafeteria _____

_____

3. The selfishness or miserliness of a certain man _____

_____

4. The wealth of a family _____

_____

5. The hospitality of a group of people _____

_____

6. The condition of county roads _____

_____

7. The generosity of a certain man _____

_____

Take one of these topics and write a tall tale based on your statement about it. Your tall tale should be like other stories; that is, it should have one or more main characters, a plot (although it doesn't have to be complicated) and a setting. The setting can be in the present, future or past. Don't make your exaggerations too fantastic.

Lesson 21
Click, Hiss, Honk and Coo
Inventing Imitative Words

Teacher Tips

Onomatopoetic words are rarely misunderstood. From *boom* to *thump* to *whizz*, they immediately convey what they are meant to convey. Although they are most effective when spoken, writers use imitative words effectively also, as shown in the quotation at the beginning of the lesson.

Students are asked to play with language in this lesson by inventing echoic words for sounds that are produced by machines, weather and pets. They should only supply one word for each category because it's a challenging job to make up words that haven't already been used to imitate these sounds.

Evaluating Responses

Among the older songs that have onomatopoetic words are:

- "Zing Go the Strings of My Heart"
- "Boo-Hoo"
- "The Trolley Song" ("Clang, clang, clang went the trolley")
- "Shoo-Fly Pie"
- "Busy as a Bee" ("I'm buzz, buzz, buzzin'")

Targeted Outcomes

- Learn the meaning of *onomatopoeia*.
- Invent words for sounds produced by machines, weather and pets.

58   TLC10563 Copyright © Teaching & Learning Company, Carthage, IL 62321-0010

Name_____

Click, Hiss, Honk and Coo

Lesson 21
Onomatopoeia

More than a century ago a music critic used these words (and others) to lambaste the tone poem "Ein Heldenleben" by Richard Strauss:

> The Hero's antagonists are described by him with the utmost scorn as a lot of pygmies and snarling, yelping, bowwowing nincompoops.

At least two of the words used by the critic were examples of onomatopoeia, the formation of words in imitation of natural sounds. Those words are *snarling* and *bowwowing*, the latter word the critic seems to have made up. Since his job was to describe musical performances, *bowwowing* appears to have been a suitable adjective for his purposes.

Because man's first attempt to invent language must have included many words that were imitations of familiar sounds, undoubtedly words such as *click, hiss, peep, coo, buzz, slurp, swish* and *quack* were among the earliest. Inasmuch as these words immediately communicate their meaning by the sounds they make, they are still highly useful today.

Find three or more songs such as "Pop Goes the Weasel" that contain onomatopoetic words.

_____

_____

_____

_____

_____

Maybe there are still words to be invented that imitate sounds. See if you can come up with at least one for each of the following categories:

machines _____

weather _____

pets _____

Lesson 22

Part or Whole?
Identifying a Synecdoche

Teacher Tips

Perhaps the most difficult thing about the device of synecdoche is pronouncing it: "sin-eck-da-kee." The term encompasses more than the two main uses that we ascribe to it in this lesson. It can also be applied to expressions in which the thing something is made of is used for the thing itself, as in *copper* for *penny*. In addition to trying to pronounce *synecdoche*, your students are to identify three examples of the device in a passage about a boy's early seagoing experiences.

Evaluating Responses

Synecdoche occurs in these places in the passage on page 61:

1. "All hands on deck!" This is part-to-whole, "hands" being a part of the body.
2. "... started earning your own bread." This is also part-to-whole, since "bread" is only a part of one's diet (that is, making a living).
3. "... soccer match between Brazil and England." This is whole-to-part because "Brazil" and "England" are countries instead of Brazilian and English national teams.

Targeted Outcomes

- Learn the definition of *synecdoche*.
- Identify three examples of the device in a passage about a boy who has gone to sea.

TLC10563 Copyright © Teaching & Learning Company, Carthage, IL 62321-0010

Name_____

Part or Whole?

Lesson 22
Synecdoche

Although we hear the device used fairly often and also use it in our speech, **synecdoche** (sin-eck-da-kee) is not a term that is familiar to most of us. **It's a figure of speech which has a part of something used to indicate a whole or, conversely, a whole used to indicate a part.** An example of the first kind of synecdoche is the use of *crown* for king or queen, as in "He swore allegiance to the crown." The other kind of synecdoche is used in this sentence: "'Here comes the law,' warned Jimmy the Dip." *Law* stands for the police force, but the speaker was referring to only one police officer.

The following paragraph has three synecdoches for you to find. Write the synecdoches below the paragraph and indicate whether each one is a "whole for a part" or a "part for a whole" type of synecdoche.

"All hands on deck!" the quartermaster roared. It was times such as this that Jeremy could hear his father's words on that last day of freedom at home: "It's time you started earning your own bread, my boy." That was only a week ago, and now he'd never know how the big soccer match between Brazil and England turned out. He didn't have a radio, and the captain sure wouldn't tell Jeremy how it turned out, even if the skipper did have a radio.

1. _____

2. _____

3. _____

Lesson 23

Not Bad
Identifying and Composing Litotes

Teacher Tips

We use the device of litotes (lih-toh-tees) so often that we don't think of it as a figure of speech. "Not bad!" we say when something impresses us. Similarly, we don't say "That's not half-good" when we approve of something but "That's not half-bad." The example of a series of litotes at the beginning of the lesson isn't really exaggerated—we often talk that way.

Evaluating Responses

The two tasks of the lesson are to identify three litotes in a passage about a freckle-faced boy and to write a paragraph containing two examples of the figure of speech. These are the three litotes in the passage on page 63. They can be paraphrased in the ways indicated below, but those aren't the only ways to do so.

1. "Kerry didn't exactly stand out in a crowd"—Kerry easily blended in with the other people in a crowd.

2. "It wasn't long . . ."—Soon.

3. ". . . his was not a run-of-the-mill pimply complexion"—He had a most unusual complexion.

Targeted Outcomes

- Identify three litotes in a passage about a freckle-faced boy.
- Write a paragraph containing two litotes.

Name_____

Not Bad

Lesson 23
Litotes

I especially noticed her in the crowd. She was not skinny, not too tall, not bad to look at and definitely not male. She was an agreeable sight.

The above is an exaggerated example of the literary device of **litotes, a negative expression that really infers the opposite of what is said or written.**

You've probably heard someone say, "That's not at all bad," meaning "That's darned good." "It wasn't unusual to see him jogging to school" means "It was common to see him jogging to school." This is another example of the use of litotes in our speaking and writing.

Identify three examples of litotes in the following passage. Underline them, write the expressions with litotes below and then paraphrase each expression so that it's positive instead of negative.

> A shy, introverted boy, Kerry didn't exactly stand out in a crowd. He wore the same clothes as the other guys, was average in size and never drew attention to himself. It wasn't long before people began to notice Kerry, however, because of his freckles. He had a million of them! They were so numerous that you didn't make them out if Kerry was 20 feet away. But when you got close, you could see that his was not a run-of-the-mill pimply complexion.

1. _____
2. _____
3. _____

Lesson 24

One Mixed-Up Man
Translating Spoonerisms
Formulating Spoonerisms

Teacher Tips

This lesson is a change of pace from those where students strain their brains dealing with figures of speech. A spoonerism is considered a figure of speech, but people don't deliberately try to insert one in their conversation. (They don't occur naturally in writing.) Students should experience some amusement in translating and formulating spoonerisms in this lesson.

Evaluating Responses

Students shouldn't have too much trouble "untransposing" the seven spoonerisms by the professor on page 65. Once they get the hang of it, they should also be able to produce five or more spoonerisms of their own. These are the translations of the professor's expressions:

1. "This class isn't all fun and games, you know."
2. "That tickles my funny bone."
3. "She always tried to make the house spick and span."
4. "It was raining cats and dogs that night."
5. "They went outside to play hide and seek."
6. "I'm going home to get a hot lunch today."
7. "No TV last night—had a short circuit."

Targeted Outcomes

- Translate seven spoonerisms.
- Formulate five original spoonerisms.

64

TLC10563 Copyright © Teaching & Learning Company, Carthage, IL 62321-0010

Name_____

Lesson 24
Spoonerisms
One Mixed-Up Man

A. We often tie two things together when we talk, using expressions such as "sugar and spice" and "fine and dandy." The professor, a teacher who is notorious for transposing his words, is quite prone to mix up these kinds of expressions. For instance, he once referred to two students as "Connie and Blyde." Another time he referred to his brother-in-law, an outdoorsman, as "Jingle Jum."

Here are some of the professor's more memorable remarks. Try to put them together as they were before he got them mixed up. They almost make sense as they are, but "untransposing" them will reveal what he really intended to say.

1. "This class isn't all guns and fame, you know." _____

2. "That tickles my bunny phone." _____

3. "She always tried to make the house spack and spin." _____

4. "It was raining cots and dags that night." _____

5. "They went outside to play side and heek." _____

6. "I'm going home to get a lot hunch today." _____

7. "No TV last night—had a shirt socket." _____

B. See if you can come up with five or more mixed-up expressions like the ones above. (Warning: This kind of talk is catching!) Have a friend decipher what you really meant.

_____
_____
_____
_____
_____

Lesson 25

Jake's Fright
Recognizing Spoonerisms
Writing a Paragraph with Two Spoonerisms

Teacher Tips

For this lesson it's assumed that students have previously done "One Mixed-Up Man" as well as the lesson about alliteration. Spoonerisms aren't to be taught, of course—they just occur unbidden to people. Their use here is simply to encourage students to write humorously. It isn't hard to think up spoonerisms after several are given. In fact, it can be a little dangerous because once you've uttered a half-dozen or more spoonerisms, it's easy to have one slip into your conversation.

Evaluating Responses

If the student spots all six spoonerisms on page 67 and corrects them, this is what his or her paper should look like:

Little Jake crept down the hall for his nightly <u>trilight twist</u> *(twilight trist)* with ice cream in the kitchen. His <u>tony ties</u> *(tiny toes)* stuck out of his <u>slippery sloppers</u> *(sloppy slippers)* because there were holes in them. However, no one seemed to stir in the house. Maybe Jake's father was not sleeping soundly because he'd gotten <u>new nose</u> *(no news)* about the <u>pendant patting</u> *(patent pending)* for his invention, but no sound came from his parents' bedroom.

"Hey, what's that?" Jake said to himself as he entered the kitchen. Oh, it was only a very big poster of a grizzly bear that his sister had taped on the side of the refrigerator. "That thing is too realistic!" Jake exclaimed to himself. And then Jake opened the refrigerator door, <u>fooling feelish</u> *(feeling foolish)*.

Targeted Outcomes

- Identify six spoonerisms in a short story.
- Incorporate two spoonerisms in a paragraph.

Name_____

Jake's Fright

Lesson 25

Spoonerisms, Alliteration

The following story contains six spoonerisms that are also alliterations. Rewrite the story by changing the spoonerisms to the expressions that the speaker intended to say. Underline the transpositions, and then write the intended words above them.

Little Jake crept down the hall for his nightly trilight twist with ice cream in the kitchen. His tony ties stuck out of his slippery sloppers because there were holes in them. However, no one seemed to stir in the house. Maybe Jake's father was not sleeping soundly because he'd gotten new nose about the pendant patting for his invention, but no sound came from his parents' bedroom.

"Hey, what's that?" Jake said to himself as he entered the kitchen. Oh, it was only a very big poster of a grizzly bear that his sister had taped on the side of the refrigerator. "That thing is too realistic!" Jake exclaimed to himself. And then Jake opened the refrigerator door, fooling feelish.

Spoonerisms are slips of the tongue and are almost never written intentionally. It is very unlikely that even Reverend W.A. Spooner, after whom the mixed-up talk was named, would have put the transpositions in written sentences. Write a paragraph of five or more sentences and slip in two spoonerisms just for fun. Try to make one of the spoonerisms alliterative.

_____

_____

_____

_____

_____

Repeaters
Identifying Tautologies

Lesson 26

Teacher Tips

"Repeaters" is comprised of an introduction, which gives the definition of a *tautology* and an example of one plus a brief passage containing two tautologies. If students are unfamiliar with the term, discuss the example given in the lesson.

The Lesson

Activities that can accompany the lesson:

Verbal-Linguistic Intelligence: The obvious and practical thing to do with this lesson is to have students try to detect tautologies in their own writing and in the writing of classmates. Although it's not likely that they will find a tautology in their own writing, the activity will make them more aware of the form and logic of their sentences.

Have students analyze the last sentence in "A Girl's Lament" on page 69. How can it be expressed without the repetition? Will it be as effective—or more effective—if it is changed?

Logical-Mathematical Intelligence: Pose this question: How can a tautology be expressed symbolically? For instance, is it simply a matter of "1 x 1 = 1"? It can't be "1 + 1 = 1," of course.

Interpersonal Intelligence: A group of three or four students can work at composing tautologies, perhaps using as subject matter some concept that's currently being studied (erosion, reciprocity, water conservation, equal rights, equilibrium, immigration laws, overpopulation or others).

Interpersonal Intelligence: Have students record their reactions to the tautology given at the beginning of the lesson after you have told them that the quotation is ancient.

Visual-Spatial Intelligence: To involve students with artistic talent, you might invite any who wish to draw a picture of the girl in the story to do so; they should also give her a name.

Evaluating Responses

It should be fairly easy for students to identify the tautology in the story ("I'm searching for happiness because I want to find happiness in my life.").

Targeted Outcomes

- Learn the definition of *tautology*.
- Identify two tautologies in the story, "A Girl's Lament."

Name_____

Repeaters

When Paul was reading a thick book, he came upon this sentence: "But everything exposed by the light becomes visible, for it is light that makes everything visible." Paul stopped reading and thought, "Huh! Isn't that double-talk? The sentence says the same thing twice."

Paul was correct. That sentence is an example of a **tautology, a needless repetition of an idea in a different word or phrase**. Sometimes we deliberately repeat a word or phrase for emphasis, but there are times when we simply become a little entangled in our words and repeat an idea without being aware we're doing it. One way of avoiding tautologies is to re-read what you have written and see if the phraseology is to the point and clear.

The following passage contains a tautology. Identify it and then underline it.

A Girl's Lament

I'd like to be an easygoing, happy-go-lucky girl, but I'm not. I like everything tidy and in its place, but the members of my family are careless—no, they're just plain sloppy. It gets me down. It's a losing battle trying to keep everything in the house presentable. If we have guests, the others shuffle things around, but the place isn't really neat. It never is! Maybe I can find an interest that will make me forget my troubles. I'm searching for happiness because I want to find happiness in my life.

Lesson 27

Game Shows
Identifying and Composing Malapropisms

Teacher Tips

As a literary device the malapropism is generally limited to times when a writer wants to inject humor into dialogue or wishes to portray a character as being prone to come up with a revealing gaffe. This lesson is principally concerned with making students aware of the device as they will rarely use it in their writing.

Evaluating Responses

These are the malaprops and the words the student really wanted to use in the talk about game shows on page 71:

> constituents—contestants
> apprized—comprised
> exhibitors—exhibitionists
> proclamation—provocation
> squib—quip
> constituents—contestants
> churlish—childish

Targeted Outcomes

- Identify seven malapropisms in a passage about televised game shows.
- Compose two malapropisms in one or two paragraphs with dialogue.

Name_____

Game Shows

The following passage contains a tautology. Identify it and then underline it.

Game Shows

Although I don't watch game shows on television much, I think I get the idea. The first requirement of a game show is that what the constituents do is not too hard. If they can't get the answers right part of the time, the show will soon be cancelled. The second requirement is that the studio audience be apprized of mostly exhibitors who scream and clap at the slightest proclamation. The last requirement is that the people who conduct the show be attractive and glib. That is, the host and/or hostess should be good-looking and quick with a squib.

The whole idea is for people at home to get hooked on the game because they can answer some of the questions and feel a little superior to the excited constituents on the show and at the same time get caught up in the churlish goings-on.

Write a brief one- or two-paragraph story and include two malapropisms used by characters in the story.

Lesson 28

Abbreviations
Deciphering Acronyms

Teacher Tips

Although there have been acronyms in American speech and writing for a very long time, they have never been as popular as they are now. Young people use acronyms, so the device will be familiar to students. One or two of the acronyms to be deciphered may be hard to get exactly right, but all of the 10 are in everyday use throughout the country.

Evaluating Responses

The 10 acronyms to be deciphered on page 74 are:

1. SWAT—special weapons and tactics
2. DOT—Department of Transportation
3. PAT—point after touchdown
4. IRA—individual retirement account
5. COLA—cost of living allowance
6. WASP—white Anglo-Saxon protestant; Woman's Air Force Service Pilots
7. ERA—earned run average; Equal Rights Amendment
8. AIDS—acquired immune deficiency syndrome
9. RIP—rest in peace
10. WAVES—women appointed for voluntary emergency service (the women's branch of the U.S. Navy)

Abbreviations
Deciphering Acronyms

Lesson 28

These are additional acronyms students might think of:

MADD—Mothers Against Drunk Driving

NOW—National Organization for Women

AWOL—absent without official leave

IRS—Internal Revenue Service

WAC—Women's Army Corps

WRENS—Women's Royal Naval Service (British)

NASA—National Aeronautics and Space Administration

NASDAQ—National Association of Securities Dealers Automated Quotation System

JAG—Judge Advocate General

NASCAR—National Association for Stock Car Auto Racing

Targeted Outcomes

- Decipher 10 common acronyms.
- List 10 additional acronyms that are used today.

Name _____

Lesson 28
Acronyms

Abbreviations

A. In an effort to save time or space, we often use **acronyms** in our speech and writing. **An acronym is a word formed by the initial letters of a name or by combining initial letters or parts of words.** The habit of using acronyms instead of the words they stand for has become more popular in recent years. Rarely does anyone say "Internal Revenue Service," especially in March or April. We say "IRS."

The origin of some acronyms is actually unknown to the great majority of people, as in the cases of *radar* for "radio detecting and ranging" and *Fiat* for the Italian car "Fabbricato Italia Automobilia Torina."

The practice in writing is to use the words that the acronym stands for at the beginning of a discussion and then to use only the acronym after. Sometimes, if the acronym is not familiar, a reader has to go back to the beginning to read what it stands for in order to understand what the acronym means.

B. What do these acronyms stand for? If you don't know, look them up.

1. SWAT _____

2. DOT _____

3. PAT _____

4. IRA _____

5. COLA _____

6. WASP _____

7. ERA _____

8. AIDS _____

9. RIP _____

10. WAVES _____

Name _____

Abbreviations

Lesson 28
Acronyms

C. Find at least 10 additional acronyms that are commonly used and give their definitions.

_____

_____

_____

_____

_____

_____

_____

_____

_____

_____

_____

_____

_____

_____

_____

_____

_____

_____

_____

_____

Lesson 29
What Does It Mean?
Interpreting Statements in Figurative Language

Teacher Tips

There are two tasks for students in this lesson. First, they are to interpret the 12 statements on pages 78-79, giving explanations of their meanings. The statements vary from the straightforward to the obscure. Second, students are to name the figure of speech that each statement exemplifies. This task is a review of the rhetorical devices presented in previous lessons. We list the figures of speech, and to some degree it will be a matter of matching. The most difficult statement to identify is the tautology.

Evaluating Responses

These are our interpretations of the statements:

1. When the chickens come home to roost, that is, when deeds come back to haunt us, there should be caution taken because we may get clobbered. This is an **epigram** because it is taking a well-known saying ("when the chickens come home to roost") and adding a witty ending.

2. No hint of wrongdoing transpired in the proceedings. "Not a breath of scandal" is giving a human characteristic (breath) to an abstraction (scandal), and so this device is **personification**.

3. Most people assume that a painter's cold hands would be more troublesome than his or her feet, but this statement indicates that the painter is chilled and is in an environment not conducive to painting. That statement is **ambiguous** because you can interpret it literally or figuratively.

4. A famous statement, this means that when you are older you can recognize the advantages of youth to a greater degree, and that young people often squander their opportunities. It is **ironic** because one would expect that young people are the ones to benefit from being young.

5. As is generally recognized, leisure lends spice to a working life. This is a simple **analogy** (work/leisure: spaghetti/sauce).

6. The speaker meant to say "merry bunch," but "berry munch" makes some kind of sense. The transposition of the initial sounds makes this a **spoonerism**.

7. For much of modern history the Irish have felt bitterness toward the British because they have felt oppressed. For them to imitate the British is surprising. This inconsistency is one of the characteristics of **irony**.

8. The person's face is so ugly that it would stop a clock—or make everyone pause in wonder. This exaggerated way of speaking and writing is called **hyperbole**.

What Does It Mean?
Interpreting Statements in Figurative Language

Lesson 29

9. We keep discovering over and over again beauties of nature and the verities of life. The **paradox** is found in the word *discover*. We seem to have to discover these things again as if they are new to us.

10. It should be clear to all of us how one becomes successful (hard work, planning ahead, "going the extra mile" and so on) since we have been told these things since childhood, but it is hard to follow these pieces of advice. The **metaphor** is found in the phrase "stepping-stones to success" inasmuch as there really are no physical stepping-stones to see; one thing is called another.

11. "Robert" is exceedingly slow because it's cold in January and molasses doesn't usually flow when being processed then. This is a familiar **simile** that compares a slowpoke to the movement of molasses in a cold month.

12. Another way to put it is that we can only know what is false by knowing what is true. This statement is a **tautology** because it seems to repeat itself.

Targeted Outcomes
- Explain the meaning of 12 statements.
- Determine what figures of speech the statements are.

Name_____

What Does It Mean?

Lesson 29
Figurative Language

A. Hardly a day goes by that you don't hear a familiar saying that makes a comment about life. "When it rains it pours," "When the going gets tough, the tough get going" and "Let the chips fall where they may" are expressions we hear all the time. We instantly understand their meaning. There are other expressions, however, that can cause us to ponder a bit. The statements that follow might make you think twice (or three times). Explain each one to the best of your ability.

1. _____ When the chickens come home to roost, make sure there's no fox waiting in the hen house. _____
_____

2. _____ There was not a breath of scandal involved in the proceedings. _____
_____
_____

3. _____ It is impossible to paint well when your feet are cold. _____
_____

4. _____ Youth is wasted on the young. _____
_____

5. _____ Work is related to leisure in the same way that spaghetti is related to sauce.
_____
_____

6. _____ "That's a berry munch," Chet said as he looked over at the wedding party.
_____
_____

7. _____ In doing this, Ireland was actually imitating England, the nation she most hated. _____
_____

Name_____ **Lesson 29**
What Does It Mean? *Figurative Language*

8. _____ His face would stop a clock. _____

_____

_____

9. _____ We repeatedly discover what is familiar to us. _____

_____

_____

10. _____ The stepping-stones to success are there for anyone to see, but most of

us don't bother to look for them. _____

_____

11. _____ "Robert's as slow as molasses in January," complained his father. _____

_____

_____

12. _____ To sort out the truth from data or circumstances requires that we establish

what is true first. _____

_____

B. The statements above are also examples of figures of speech. Among them you should recognize:

a simile
a metaphor
an ambiguity
a paradox
a spoonerism
two ironies
a personification
a hyperbole
an epigram
a tautology
analogy

Indicate the figure of speech to the left of each statement.